North Star Numbers

A Minnesota Number Book

Written by Kathy-jo Wargin and Illustrated by Laurie Caple

Tonka is a trademark of Hasbro and is used with permission.
© 2007 Hasbro. All Rights Reserved.

The illustrator would like to thank Glen Livermont of the Pipestone National Monument; Matthew G. Anderson, Curator, Minnesota Historical Society; Matt Dacy, Department of Development of the Mayo Clinic; the Mill City Museum; Jeff Boorom and Tom Lalim of Historical Fort Snelling; Patrick Schifferdecker, Site Manager North West Company Fur Post; and the Greyhound Bus Origin Museum.

Sleeping Bear Press™

310 North Main Street, Suite 300
Chelsea, MI 48118
www.sleepingbearpress.com

© 2008 Sleeping Bear Press is an imprint of Gale, a part of Cengage Learning.

Printed and bound in China.

First Edition

10 9 8 7 6 5 4 3 2 1

Library of Congress Cataloging-in-Publication Data

Wargin, Kathy-jo.
North Star numbers : a Minnesota number book / written by Kathy-jo Wargin; illustrated by Laurie Caple.
p. cm.
Summary: "Using simple number concepts, North Star Numbers: A Minnesota Number Book takes readers back in time to experience nineteenth century army life at Fort Snelling, miles of canoe routes, and find out where thousands of bright yellow Tonka Trucks were made"—Provided by publisher.
ISBN 978-1-58536-187-8
1. Minnesota—Juvenile literature. 2. Counting—Juvenile literature.
I. Caple, Laurie A., ill. II. Title.

F606.3.W365 2008
977.6—dc22   2007037659

To my son, Jake. You were born in Minnesota,
and will always be the number one North Star to me.

KATHY-JO

★

For Cindy Cragg and Lori Gray—
treasured friends I can always count on!

LAURIE

For thousands of years, American Indians came to the area we now call southwestern Minnesota to quarry a soft red stone known as pipestone or catlinite. The pipes and artifacts carved out of this unique stone became sacred objects and valuable trading goods. To the nations of Ojibwa, Pawnee, Sac, Fox, Lakota, and others, these grounds became a sacred and peaceful place. In 1937 the U.S. Congress designated the site as a national monument, which we know today as Pipestone National Monument.

1 reddish peace pipe.
It's sacred and known
as a beautiful symbol
that's carved out of stone.

one

1

The Métis (MAY-tee) carried their furs from Canada, North Dakota, or the Red River Valley to St. Paul in a simple two-wheel cart known as the oxcart. Riding in caravans known as "trains," they sometimes traveled in groups of more than 100 carts. Once they reached St. Paul and furs were unloaded, these carts were filled for a return trip with goods such as tobacco, cloth, food, and guns. The furs brought to St. Paul during this time made the city one of the leading fur markets in the country from the 1840s to the 1860s. By the turn of the century, the oxcart was seldom seen because steam boats and railroads had become more common.

two

2

2 Red River oxcarts,
a good way to haul
heavy furs from the north
to the town of St. Paul.

When a tornado swept through Rochester in 1883, Dr. William W. Mayo and his sons, Dr. William J. and Dr. Charles H., were requested to help build the St. Mary's Hospital, which opened in 1889. As medical needs grew, the doctors Mayo invited other specialists to work with them, creating a model for group practice. By 1914 a new clinic was completed, and officially named the Mayo Clinic. Today the Mayo Clinic is known as one of the leading medical facilities in the world.

three

3

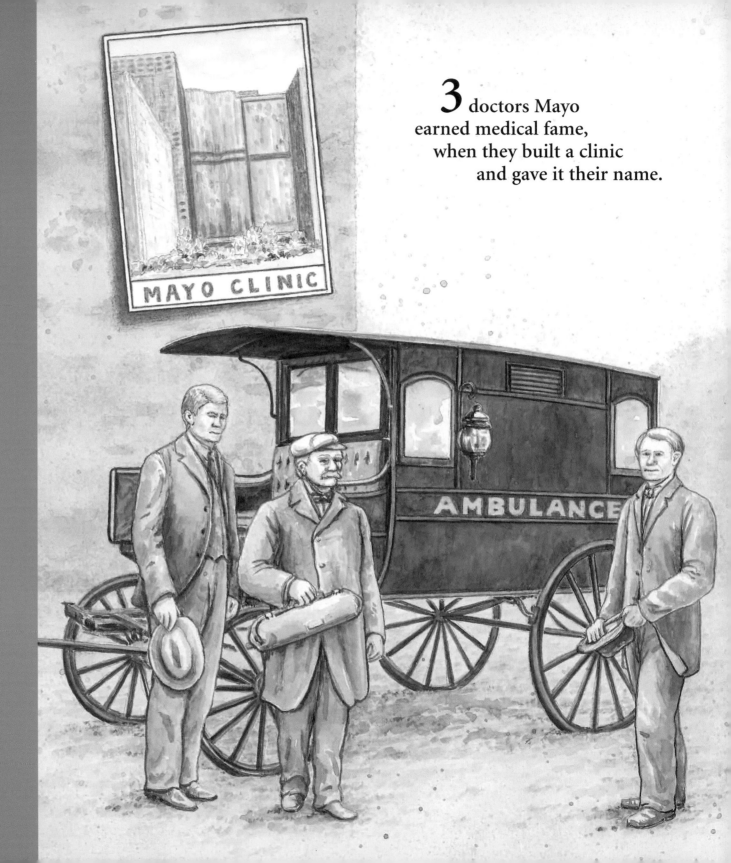

3 doctors Mayo
earned medical fame,
when they built a clinic
and gave it their name.

The monarch butterfly is the official state butterfly of Minnesota. Bright orange and black, they are commonly seen in the backyards and open spaces of the state. Monarchs are 3 to 4.5 inches (7.5–11.5 cm) long and weigh less than one ounce (28 g). Monarch larvae eat only milkweed, while mature monarchs eat the nectar of various flowering plants. Every summer there are approximately four generations of monarchs born in Minnesota. In the fall most monarch butterflies migrate south to Mexico and California. In the spring they fly north again to continue the cycle.

four

4

4 little monarchs
adrift in the sun,
or resting on milkweed—
can you count each one?

5 hockey players,
each ready to skate.
The heroes of hockey
belong in our state!

Minnesota has a rich tradition of successful hockey players and institutions. Because of this, the United States Hockey Hall of Fame is located in Eveleth, Minnesota and honors the sport through its displays and memorabilia. Eveleth is also home to the world's largest hockey stick and puck. In 1967 a National Hockey League expansion franchise was awarded to Minnesota for the Minnesota North Stars. In 1993 the franchise was moved to Dallas and renamed the Dallas Stars. In 1997 the NHL granted another franchise to Minnesota, which is known as the Minnesota Wild.

five

5

6 beautiful gray wolves
with coats gray and black.
They live in the north woods
and run in a pack.

Minnesota is home to the largest wolf population in the lower 48 states. Gray Wolves, or *Canis lupus*, are commonly referred to as timber wolves, and weigh between 70 to 100 pounds (31.5 to 45 kg). These large mammals have strong jaws and legs, bushy tails, and are typically various shades of gray to black, although some individual wolves may be solid black, reddish, or buff colored. Wolves thrive in the deep forest areas of northern Minnesota, and because of this, their habits have been the focus of intense wolf studies for many decades.

Wolves live in a pack, which is a family group that consists of adult mates and their young. Packs are typically between 6 to 12 wolves. This makes it easier for the wolves to be successful at hunting prey, which usually consists of deer, moose, or small mammals. The International Wolf Center in Ely promotes public awareness and education about wolves.

six

6

Minneapolis was once known as the "Flour Milling Capital of the World." By the 1850s, flour mills were being established on many rivers and creeks. The city of Minneapolis grew up and around the milling area, and by 1870 had a population of 13,000 people. There were 12 mills in operation along the powerful St. Anthony Falls, the only significant waterfall on the Mississippi River. Grain for milling was brought to the city by trains coming in from the West and Canada, and in return, milled flour was shipped out in sacks to Duluth and eastern United States destinations. As the area and industry grew, the Minneapolis Riverfront earned its reputation as the flour milling center, leading the world in flour production, an honor the area held until 1930.

seven

7

7 big flour sacks
    set in the train.
We milled the most
of such flour from grain.

In 1819 the junction of the Mississippi and Minnesota Rivers was an important waterway. To ensure that illegal fur traders did not exploit this important asset, the 5th Regiment of Infantry came to build a fort as part of a chain of forts being built to protect the valuable waterways. Fort Snelling was completed in 1825 under the watch of Colonel Josiah Snelling. His officers made roads, built a gristmill, a sawmill at St. Anthony Falls, planted produce, and raised livestock, all while upholding the laws and policies of the United States. Fort Snelling remained the center of the Upper Mississippi for nearly 30 years, and was a meeting place for many cultures such as the Dakota and Ojibwe, French fur traders, and European settlers. In 1960 the U.S. Department of the Interior designated Fort Snelling as the state's first National Historic Landmark.

eight
8

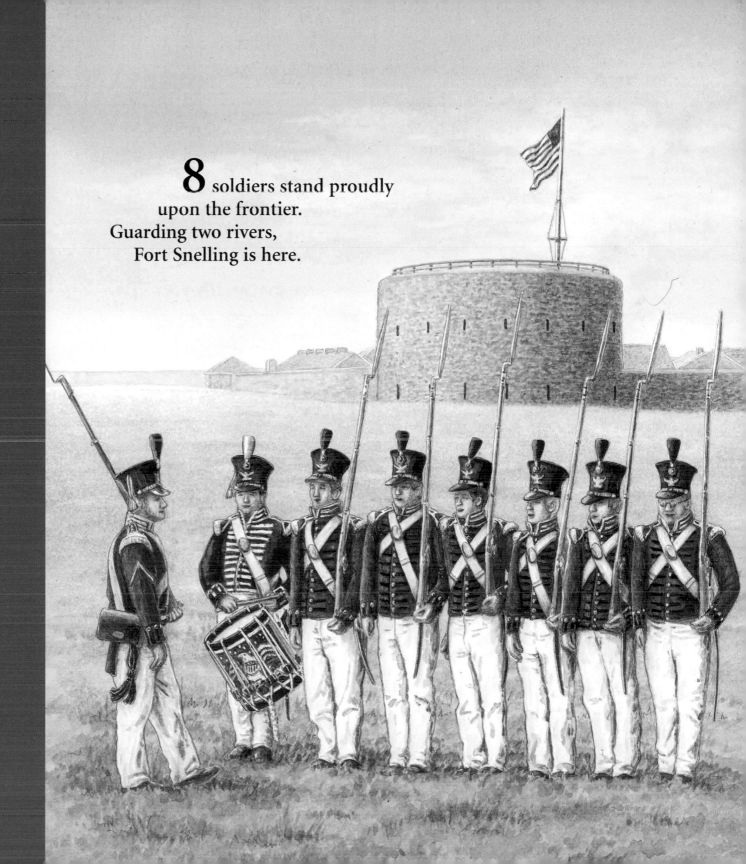

8 soldiers stand proudly upon the frontier.
Guarding two rivers,
Fort Snelling is here.

9 friends of the prairie,
    our state is their home.
The American bison
        remains here to roam.

Minnesota's vast prairie was an ideal habitat for the American bison, which once thrived here in large herds. The Plains Indians hunted the bison for food as recent as 150 years ago, but they were careful to take only what they needed. It was the pioneers who came to settle the West who killed large numbers of bison because they didn't want them trampling over their newly acquired land. Other hunters killed the bison for sport or hides, and because of this the bison population was nearly decimated. Today, thanks to parks established to protect the bison, we have the largest population in more than 100 years. They roam freely in many state and national parks, including Blue Mounds State Park in southwestern Minnesota.

nine
9

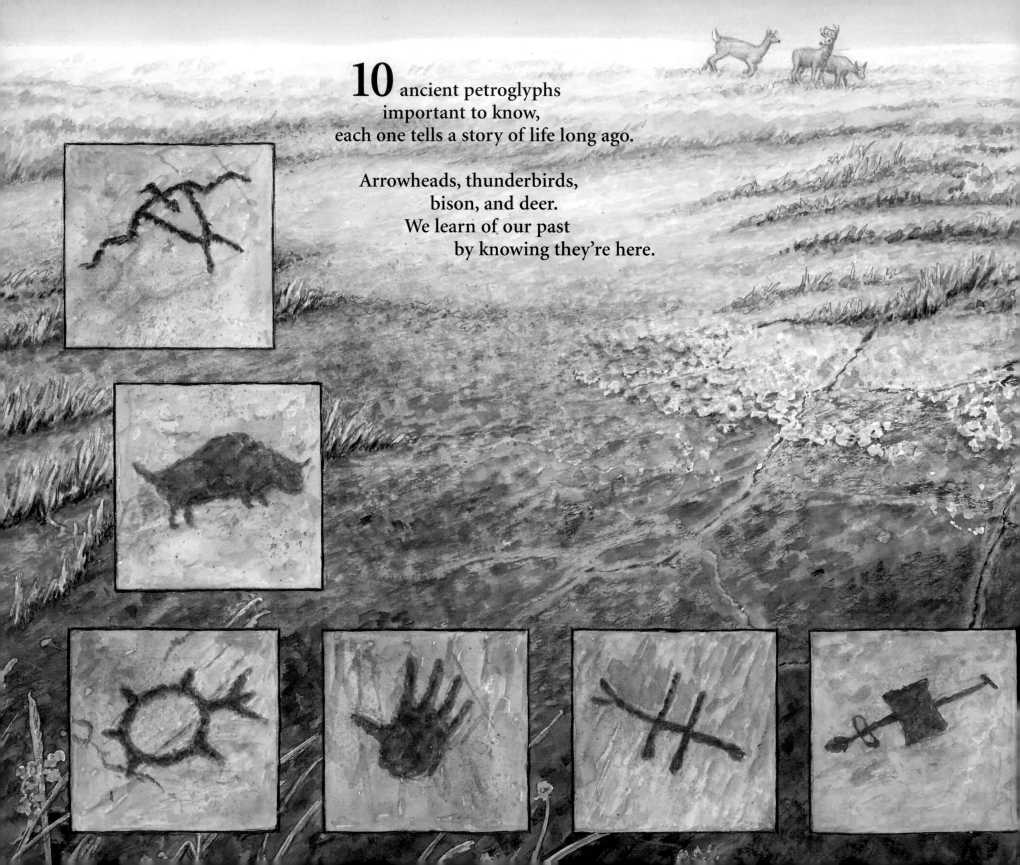

10 ancient petroglyphs
important to know,
each one tells a story of life long ago.

Arrowheads, thunderbirds,
bison, and deer.
We learn of our past
by knowing they're here.

A petroglyph is an image carved into rock. Images such as these can be found at Jeffers Petroglyphs State Historic Site in southern Minnesota. Pictures etched into outcroppings of quartzite include thunderbirds, atlatls, elk, bison, and more. These images were created by various tribes of American Indians as early as 3000 BC and were created to tell stories, record important events, and share with us what was meaningful to their lives. It is important to preserve sacred sites such as the Jeffers Petroglyphs, so that future generations may learn about the important cultures of the people who created them.

ten
10

11 morel mushrooms,
   some big and some small.
A true sign of spring,
      can you count them all?

Adopted in 1984 as the Official State Mushroom of Minnesota, the golden-colored morel mushroom, or *Morchella esculenta*, often grows in fields or forests at the base of dead cottonwood or elm trees. These cone-shaped mushrooms range from 2 to 6 inches (5 to 15 cm) high and have long, hollow, pitted caps. They are typically creamy tan or brownish and darken with age, and their spongy heads give them a unique appearance. Southeastern Minnesota has more morel mushrooms than any other part of the state. Golden-colored morel mushrooms are a tasty treat for knowledgeable mushroom hunters. As always, never eat a wild mushroom unless you have absolute verification of its identity.

eleven

11

The colorful characters of Minnesota's past include the fur traders and voyageurs. Voyageurs were men of primarily French Canadian heritage who traveled great distances in their canoes, hauling furs to trade for goods. Many traders established posts in the vast wilderness, trading goods such as cloth and beads to Native Americans and pioneer trappers in exchange for beaver furs. At special times, voyageurs would carry these furs to a meeting place or rendezvous, and exchange them for additional loads of goods, which were brought back to the wilderness so more trading for furs could be done. In Pine City, Minnesota, the North West Company Fur Post is a reconstructed trading post, located along the Snake River, which includes exhibits, guides, and a visitor center.

twelve
12

12 busy traders
at work in the North.
The best furs and goods
to exchange back and forth.

According to the Department of Natural Resources, Minnesota ranks first in the nation in regard to the number of boats, which is one for every six people. Minnesota also ranks first for the number of fishing licenses per capita. Minnesota has 158 species of fish, and more than 5,000 fishable lakes. With over 3,000 public lake access points and more than 3,000 miles (nearly 5,000 km) of canoe routes, Minnesota is a natural choice for people who love the water.

twenty

20

20 boats bobbing—
they drift and troll.
It's time to catch fish.
Let's cast and roll!

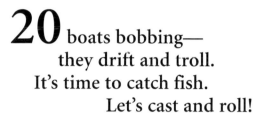

30 trucks yellow
at work on a hill.
A big load of sand
to dump, plow, and fill!

In 2004 the Tonka Truck was inducted into the National Toy Hall of Fame. Created in 1947 by a group of Minnesota teachers using pressed steel, their first toy trucks were created in the basement of a schoolhouse and included a steam shovel and crane. In the first year they sold 37,000 toys. Initially called Mound Metalcraft, the group decided to change the company name to Tonka, which is the Sioux word for "great." In 1964 they introduced the yellow Mighty Dump Truck, which became their bestselling toy truck of the century.

In 1988 the blueberry muffin was adopted as the official state muffin of Minnesota. Blueberries have always been found in Minnesota, and are one of the few fruits native to North America, which is the world's largest producer of blueberries. Of the genus *Vaccinium*, this flowering plant produces small crown shaped berries that are high in nutritional value, and are one of only a few human foods that are naturally colored blue.

Look in the basket.
Do you see the treat?
Blueberry muffins!
There's **40** to eat!

forty
40

Let's count the milk.
The glasses are filled.
Do you see all **50**?
Not one drop is spilled!

In 1984 Milk was designated as the official state drink. The dairy industry is important to Minnesota's economy, and Minnesota ranks fifth in dairy production among the states by producing more than 9 billion pounds (4 billion kg) of milk per year. Dairy processing also includes other items such as butter, cheese, ice cream, and more. One of the more popular attractions at the Minnesota State Fair is the All-You-Can-Drink Milk Stand, operated by the Minnesota Dairy Promotion Council. The average customer at the stand drinks between two and three glasses of milk.

fifty
50

In May 1914, the first "bus" began its route carrying miners to work on the Mesabi Iron Range. Carl Wickman, a Swedish miner laid off from the mine, used his Hupmobile to transport miners from Hibbing to Alice. Wickman modified his Hupmobile so that it could carry ten people and charged only fifteen cents for a one-way trip or twenty-five cents for a round trip. The bus idea was a success, but eventually Wickman was called back to the mine and sold the business to Andrew "Bus Andy" Anderson and Charles Wenberg. Over time their business became known as Greyhound Bus Lines and today, Hibbing is recognized as the birthplace of the bus industry in the United States. You can visit the Greyhound Bus Origin Museum in Hibbing.

sixty
60

60 good miners
wait without fuss.
The Hupmobile's seating
became our first bus.

HIBBING TO
ALICE 15¢

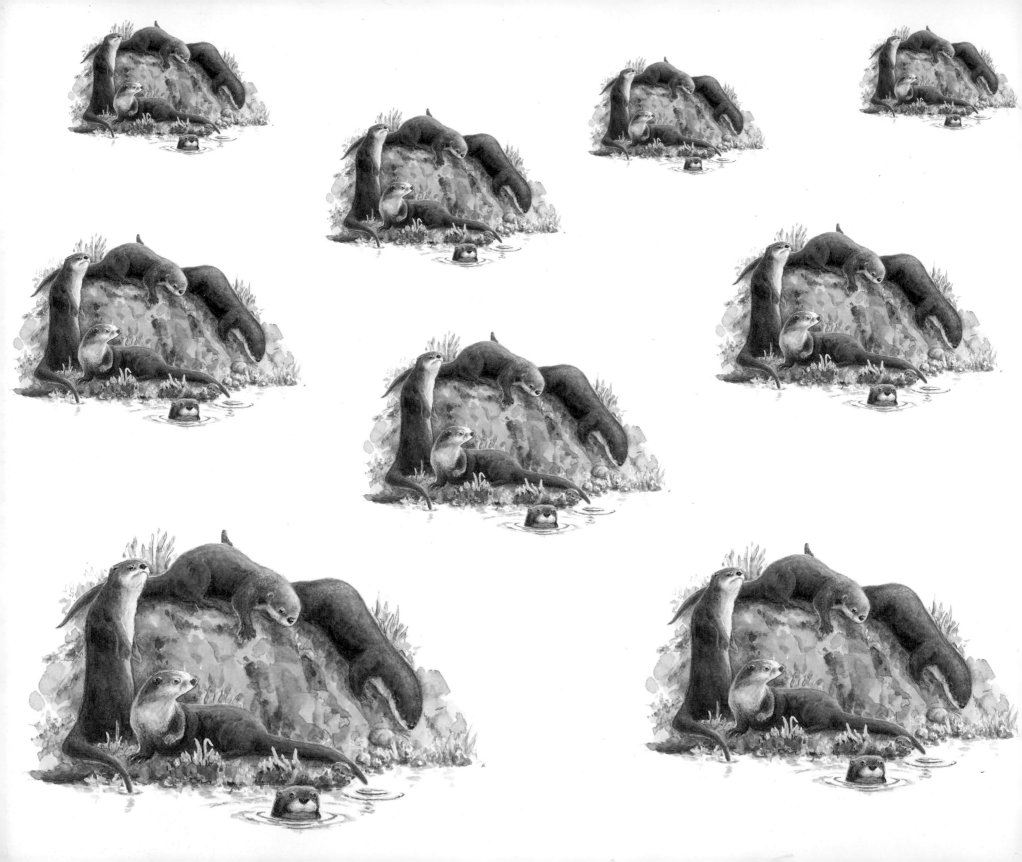

70 river otters
love to slip and slide
upon the water's muddy banks,
a twisting, turning ride!

An adult river otter is about 4 feet (122 cm) long from its nose to the tip of its tail, weighs between 20 and 30 pounds (9 and 13.5 kg), and is Minnesota's largest aquatic carnivore. The sleek, glossy brown river otter lives predominantly on the lakes, rivers, and streams of northern Minnesota, although their numbers are increasing into southern Minnesota due to wetland restoration efforts. Often recognized for its playful nature, a river otter will make up games to play as a way to practice its skills as a predator.

seventy

70

Minnesota is home to a variety of wildlife including black bears. An adult black bear weighs between 100 and 300 pounds (45 and 135 kg), and is 4.5 to 5 feet (1.4 to 1.5 m) in length. Black bears are shy and will usually try to stay away from people, but sometimes in their search for food they will cross paths with the human population. Black bears typically eat a diet rich in nuts, roots, berries, mice, insects, and fish. Originally found throughout all of Minnesota, black bears today are predominantly found in northern Minnesota. Although called the "black bear," its coat may vary from light brown to deep black.

eighty

80

80 black bears
fast asleep in the sun.
Some bears can be brown,
can you count each one?

90 lush trees—
each one stands tall
atop Eagle Mountain,
the tallest of all!

Eagle Mountain is the state's highest point at 2,301 feet (700 m) above sea level. Located in Cook County, it is part of the Boundary Waters Canoe Area Wilderness and the Misquah Hills area of the Superior National Forest. Like the rest of northeastern Minnesota, the Misquah Hills are also part of the Canadian Shield, making it one of the oldest ranges in the world. The area is a picturesque combination of paper birch, spruce, eastern white pine, red pine, balsam fir, and more as well as bogs and rocky bluffs. The area contains the Eagle Mountain Trail, a popular scenic hiking trail.

ninety
90

Also commonly called seagulls, herring gulls are a favorite sight in northern Minnesota. These large, gray-backed gulls like to nest on rocky cliffs and near coastal waters. Known to take advantage of any opportunity to eat, herring gulls will often attempt to feed on garbage or spilled food when available, although the majority of their natural diet consists of fish, earthworms, and marine invertebrates. A favorite northern destination to spot herring gulls is Split Rock Lighthouse, possibly one of the nation's most scenic lighthouses. Completed in 1909 and commissioned one year later, Split Rock Lighthouse and its keepers helped ships navigate the treacherous waters of Lake Superior for 59 years. In 1971 the lighthouse station was deeded to the State of Minnesota as a historic site.

one
hundred
100

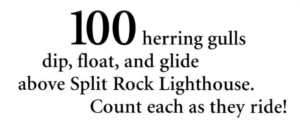

100 herring gulls
dip, float, and glide
above Split Rock Lighthouse.
Count each as they ride!

It's time for goodbye—
Count all that you see,
　for all North Star Numbers
　　begin 1–2–3!

Kathy-jo Wargin

Kathy-jo Wargin was born in Tower, Minnesota as Kathy-jo Nelson, and lived there until her family later moved to Aurora, and then to Grand Rapids, Minnesota. Today she is known for her many award-winning stories celebrating the north country including *V is for Viking: A Minnesota Alphabet, The Legend of Minnesota, The Voyageurs's Paddle, The Legend of the Loon* (an IRA Children's Choice Book), *The Legend of the Lady's Slipper* (an Upper Midwest Bookseller's Favorite), *The Edmund Fitzgerald: The Song of the Bell, B is for Badger: A Wisconsin Alphabet,* and *The Legend of Wisconsin.* She lives in Petoskey, Michigan with her family.

Laurie Caple

A childhood spent exploring the beauty and treasures of the natural world helped set the stage for Laurie Caple's career as a nature artist and children's book illustrator. She has illustrated more than a dozen books and numerous publications including *American Girl* magazine. Her first book with Sleeping Bear Press was *The Legend of Old Abe: A Civil War Eagle,* also written by Kathy-jo Wargin. A frequent presenter at elementary schools, Laurie lives in Faribault, Minnesota, with her husband and two sons.